STEM IN THE WORLD SERIES

BY MARNE VENTURA

CONTENT CONSULTANT

JESSE WILCOX, PHD

ASSISTANT PROFESSOR OF STEM EDUCATION

SIMPSON COLLEGE

SportsZone

An Imprint of Abdo Publishing
abdobooks.com

ABDOBOOKS.COM

Published by Abdo Publishing, a division of ABDO, PO Box 398166, Minneapolis, Minnesota 55439. Copyright © 2020 by Abdo Consulting Group, Inc. International copyrights reserved in all countries. No part of this book may be reproduced in any form without written permission from the publisher. SportsZone™ is a trademark and logo of Abdo Publishing.

Printed in the United States of America, North Mankato, Minnesota
092019
012020

THIS BOOK CONTAINS
RECYCLED MATERIALS

Cover Photo: Eric Christian Smith/AP Images
Interior Photos: Charlie Riedel/AP Images, 4–5, 15 (top); David J. Phillip/AP Images, 7, 15 (bottom); Matt Slocum/AP Images, 8; Godofredo A. Vasquez/Houston Chronicle/AP Images, 11; AP Images, 12–13; Mark Blinch/The Canadian Press/AP Images, 17; Eric Risberg/AP Images, 18; Bettmann/Getty Images, 20–21, 23; Shutterstock Images, 24, 35; Jamie Squire/Getty Images Sport/Getty Images, 27; Tim Roberts Photography/ Shutterstock Images, 28–29; Frank Jansky/Icon Sportswire/AP Images, 31; Tom Szczerbowski/Getty Images Sport/Getty Images, 32; Felix Mizioznikov/Shutterstock Images, 37; Omar Rawlings/Getty Images Sport/ Getty Images, 38–39; Lynne Sladky/AP Images, 41; Kyodo/AP Images, 43; Red Line Editorial, 45

Editor: Marie Pearson
Series Designer: Dan Peluso

LIBRARY OF CONGRESS CONTROL NUMBER: 2019942089

PUBLISHER'S CATALOGING-IN-PUBLICATION DATA
Names: Ventura, Marne, author.
Title: STEM in the World Series / by Marne Ventura
Description: Minneapolis, Minnesota : Abdo Publishing, 2020 | Series: STEM in the greatest sports events | Includes online resources and index.
Identifiers: ISBN 9781532190599 (lib. bdg.) | ISBN 9781644943175 (pbk.) | ISBN 9781532176449 (ebook)
Subjects: LCSH: World Series (Baseball)--Juvenile literature. | Sports sciences--Juvenile literature. | Applied science--Juvenile literature. | Baseball--Juvenile literature. | Physics--Juvenile literature.
Classification: DDC 796.015--dc23

TABLE OF CONTENTS

Dexter Fowler opened Game 7 with a home run for Chicago.

CHAPTER 1

WORLD SERIES CHAMPIONS

A sudden cloudburst released a downpour on Progressive Field in Cleveland, Ohio. It drenched the 38,000 fans in the stadium. The Chicago Cubs and the Cleveland Indians were in Game 7 of the 2016 World Series. The game had started at 8:00 pm. It was now almost midnight. After nine innings, Cleveland and Chicago were tied, 6–6. The start of the 10th inning would have to be delayed because of the rain.

The fans were on the edge of their seats. Chicago had not won the World Series in 108 years. For Cleveland, it had been 68 years. The World Series had been going on for more than a week. Of the six previous games, each team had won three. The winner of Game 7 would take this year's World Series trophy and break their team's decades-long losing streak.

After 17 minutes, the rain stopped, and the game resumed. Chicago's Kyle Schwarber hit a single. Pinch runner Albert Almora was put in for Schwarber on first base. Next, Kris Bryant hit a fly to center, and Almora got to second. Cleveland walked Anthony Rizzo, and then Ben Zobrist stepped up to the plate. Zobrist hit a double to left field. Almora scored a run, and Chicago was now ahead, leading 7–6. Next, Cleveland walked Addison Russell, and then Miguel Montero hit a single. Rizzo scored on the play. Now Chicago was ahead 8–6.

It was the bottom of the 10th inning, and Cleveland was up to bat. After two outs, they scored

Almora celebrates after scoring in the tenth inning.

a run. The score was now 8–7 Chicago. In a dramatic play, Cleveland's Michael Martinez hit a grounder. Bryant caught it and threw it to Rizzo at first before Martinez could get there. That was Cleveland's final out. Chicago became the 2016 World Series champions.

Chicago Cubs players celebrate their 2016 World Series victory.

STEM IN ACTION

The World Series is the exciting end of each year's

Major League Baseball (MLB) season. The champions of

the American League (AL) play against the champions of the National League (NL). The first team to win four out of seven games prevails. Games are split between the two teams' stadiums. The team with the best regular season record gets four home games, while the other team gets three home games. Since the first World Series in 1903, athletes, coaches, and managers have gotten better at playing and winning by using science, technology, engineering, and math (STEM). STEM is an important part of every World Series game.

Science explains a lot about what happens in the World Series. Physics can explain why an outfielder might disagree with a call made by the umpire at home plate. Scientists have done studies on whether it's best to slide headfirst or feetfirst to steal a base. A stolen base has been the difference between winning and losing a World Series.

Technology has advanced dramatically since 1903. Sports fans used to have to be at the stadium to see the game. Years later they could listen on the radio. Today microphones, cameras, and computers let baseball lovers experience the sights and sounds of the World Series even if they're not at the ballpark.

Engineers play a key role in the World Series too. MLB stadiums now include modern features such as enormous videoboards. Artificial turf saves water. Engineers design stadiums to prevent the wind from affecting the game.

Math and the World Series have been partners since the game began. Numbers decide which teams make it to the playoffs. Managers now use data and analytics in addition to scouting reports to pick players. They try to find the best players to help the team win in the regular season and reach the World Series. Math is used to figure out the best position for each player.

STEM plays a role in every part of the World Series, from how it's played to how it's managed and how it's watched. The event's traditions are more than 100 years

Understanding STEM concepts can make the World Series even more exciting to follow.

old, but the World Series continues to change because of advances in STEM fields. Science, technology, engineering, and math help make the World Series one of America's most popular sports events.

Don Larsen pitched in the major leagues for 14 years.

2

THE SCIENCE OF THE WORLD SERIES

Understanding science can help fans better understand the World Series. When a pitcher doesn't let a single player from the other team get on base, it's called a perfect game. It happened only once in World Series history. In Game 2 in 1956, the New York Yankees' Don Larsen threw 97 pitches during the game. He retired 27 Brooklyn Dodgers batters. In the entire game, the Dodgers got no hits and no walks. A perfect game is so rare that it has happened only 23 times in MLB history since 1880.

In 2010, journalist and baseball fan George Will wrote that the umpire who called Larsen's last pitch was wrong. After watching the video recording, he said the ball was 1.5 feet (0.5 m) high and outside the strike zone. Lew Paper, the author of a book about Larsen's perfect game, agreed. He wrote that Yankees outfielder Mickey Mantle and shortstop Gil McDougald both said the pitch looked like it had gone outside the strike zone.

Today most experts agree that if Larsen's last pitch wasn't a strike, it was very close. But there's a reason that people watching the pitch saw it in different ways. Alan Nathan is a professor of physics at the University of Illinois. He is an expert on the physics of baseball. Nathan has watched the video of Larsen's perfect game many times. He says that because the camera angle view of Larsen is off-center, it is affected by something called parallax. Parallax is a difference in the way an object is

Angle 1

Angle 2

These photos illustrate the parallax effect. They are of the same moment. Cleveland's Carlos Santana reaches for first base as Chicago's first baseman Anthony Rizzo tries to tag him. In the first photo, it appears as if Rizzo has tagged Santana. The second photo shows the same action from a different angle. This angle shows Santana was not tagged.

seen from two different points of view. The camera that filmed the famous pitch was above and to the first-base side. This distorts the position of the ball in the viewer's eyes. Because the umpire is standing near the batter, the way he sees a pitch is more accurate than the way viewers or players see it from distant angles.

HEADFIRST OR FEETFIRST?

David Peters is a physicist and baseball fan at Washington University. He uses physics to study the best way to slide onto a base. He says that a player's center of gravity is halfway between the tips of the fingers and the tips of the toes. The center of gravity affects the momentum. An object's speed in a certain direction multiplied by its mass is its momentum. The more massive the body and the faster the speed, the greater the momentum. When a runner slides headfirst, his center of gravity is thrust forward. With a feetfirst slide, the center of gravity falls backward, away from the base.

Sliding headfirst can help a runner touch the base faster than sliding feetfirst.

The player gets to the base slower. It's better for a runner to push his head and arms forward with his legs.

The debate about sliding has been going on since before the start of the World Series. Some coaches and players worry that sliding headfirst has a higher risk

Rickey Henderson slides into first base in Game 5 of the 1992
AL Championship Series.

of injury. But many players continue to use this method
to try to increase their chance of making it to base.

Rickey Henderson played in the major leagues from
1979 to 2003. Years after his final season, he still ranked
first all-time in runs scored (with 2,295) and stolen bases
(with 1,406). He has been nicknamed "the Man of Steal."

He helped the Oakland A's win the World Series in 1989. Then he helped the Toronto Blue Jays win it in 1993. He preferred to slide headfirst. He said he tried to dive close to the ground, like a plane landing.

In Game 4 of the 2004 AL Championship Series, the Boston Red Sox's Dave Roberts stole second base. The steal allowed the Red Sox to win and go on to the World Series, where they also won. Roberts stole the base with a headfirst slide.

A GAME OF INCHES

One study on sliding found that players who slide headfirst get to second base .02 seconds faster than feetfirst. That doesn't sound like much. But a player running 15 miles per hour (24 km/h) who slides headfirst would make it 5 inches (13 cm) farther in those .02 seconds than a player who slides feetfirst. That could be the difference between safe or out.

Fans gathered at the Huntington Avenue Grounds for the 1903 World Series.

CHAPTER 3

TECHNOLOGY IN THE WORLD SERIES

T he only way for fans to see or hear the first World Series in 1903 was to show up at the ballpark. Fans packed Huntington Avenue Grounds in Boston, Massachusetts, for Game 3. Fans who could not make it to the game had to read about it later in the newspaper.

In 1921 the World Series was broadcast on radio for the first time. The New York Giants played the New York Yankees at the Polo Grounds, which served as both teams' home field that season. Only three radio stations covered the event. Fans in Pittsburgh, Pennsylvania, heard the game live while a sportswriter announced the game. Fans in Springfield, Massachusetts, and Newark, New Jersey, heard an announcer describe the game after a colleague at the Polo Grounds phoned in reports.

VIDEO AND SOUND BROADCASTING

In 1939 two cameras broadcast an MLB game for the first time. One looked down the first-base line. The other was above home plate. This camera captured the whole diamond.

OPERATOR ERROR

Sometimes technology is limited by its operators. A single camera recorded the 1949 World Series. It was placed in right field because that's as far as the cable would reach. When Yankees player Tommy Henrich hit a game-winning home run, it flew right toward the camera. Instead of moving the camera, the operator forgot his job and tried to catch the ball. He did not track the ball with the camera.

Three men listen to a 1926 World Series game on the radio.

The first World Series to be aired on television was played in 1947. Television stations used orthicon cameras, which had wide-angle lenses in order to show the large field. They also had telephoto lenses that provided close-up views.

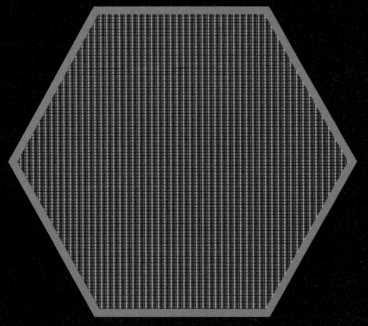

This photo shows the pixels in a liquid crystal display television. A pixel is one point of color that, with surrounding pixels, creates an image on a screen. The number of pixels influences how sharp an image looks, but there are multiple aspects that contribute to that sharpness. First, a camera must be able to record an image with a large number of pixels. The more pixels a camera records with, the larger the image can be made while still appearing sharp. Second, the screen on which the image or video is viewed must have a lot of pixels, or the image won't look sharp. A larger screen needs more pixels. A third factor in image sharpness is pixel density, or how closely the pixels are packed together. The closer the pixels are, the closer a viewer can be to the screen and have the image still appear sharp. Huge video boards at stadiums are viewed from far away. So their pixels don't need to be as tightly packed as a home television's. On these video boards, a single pixel can be as large as 1.5 inches (4 cm).

By the 1950s, broadcasters of the World Series used a camera mounted above the field. This camera could capture the whole infield at once. A new kind of camera lens allowed for up-close video of players in action. Fans became familiar with their favorite players' faces. The World Series began using more cameras. By the 1970s, most games were covered with four or five cameras.

In the 1980s, wireless microphones were positioned around the field to pick up sounds. Now, in addition to seeing the game, fans could hear the crack of the bat, the ball hitting the catcher's glove, the runner's feet pounding, and the roar of the crowd.

SKYCAM AND SUPER DUPER SLO MO

In 1984 NBC used a Super Duper Slo Mo camera that showed 90 frames per second. Live television is typically 30 or 60 frames per second. The slow motion camera replayed events in the game so that viewers could see up-close details. They could see the red stitches of the seams on the baseball as a pitch flew toward the plate.

Also in 1984, NBC-TV used the Skycam for the first time at the World Series. The camera hangs from cables above the field. The cables can reel in and out, allowing an operator to move the camera over the field. The camera can show what's happening from many angles. In time, Skycam became high definition (HD). HD cameras send images that have more pixels than standard pictures. This means the picture shows more detail. In 2002 Fox broadcast the World Series in high definition for the first time. Today Skycams are mounted higher than 20 feet (6 m) above the stands in foul territory. The cameras move along the base paths. Skycams capture overhead views of the action. The computer-controlled camera can zoom, pan, and tilt.

World Series technology continues to improve. Fans can watch many angles of a play, get a sharper picture than ever before, and feel more and more like they are part of the game.

Some cameras in the World Series are handheld.

Chase Field's retractable roof was carefully designed by engineers.

4

ENGINEERING THE WORLD SERIES

I n the past, MLB and National Football League (NFL) events sometimes used the same stadiums. Today many new ballparks have been built just for MLB. Engineers design ballparks with special features for hosting World Series games.

Chase Field is the home of the Arizona Diamondbacks. Built in 1998, it hosted four World Series games in 2001. It was the first domed US ballpark with a retractable roof. A retractable roof can be opened up.

Phoenix is very hot in the summer. It has sudden storms. The retractable roof is made of 9 million pounds (4 million kg) of steel. The roof is made of two pieces that can be pulled back from each other. A pair of motors opens or closes the roof in slightly more than four minutes. Either side of the roof can be opened to any position. When the weather is mild, the roof can stay open for games. In heat or rain, it closes. The ballpark is also air-conditioned.

Fans in a stadium may be far from the athletes on the field. Engineers are designing bigger and better video boards to help fans see the game in close-up detail. Video boards also display the score and information about the players. In 2008 the average MLB stadium video board was 2,600 square feet (240 sq m). By 2016 the average video board was 8,000 square feet (740 sq m). In 2019 the largest MLB stadium board was at Cleveland's Progressive Field. The screen is 221 feet (67 m) wide by 59 feet (18 m) tall. That's more than 13,000 square feet (1,200 sq m) of high-definition video.

Progressive Field's giant video board can keep fans up to date on stats and plays.

Progressive Field had this video board installed before it hosted games in the 2016 World Series.

THE TURF DEBATE

Artificial turf, or fake grass, was first used in the Houston Astrodome in 1966. By the 1990s, 10 MLB parks used

Artificial turf can look very similar to real grass, but it doesn't play the same.

artificial turf. The fake grass was like a carpet made from

fabric. Most players at the time preferred natural grass.

They worried that the chance of injury was greater when

playing on artificial grass. MLB stadiums stopped using artificial turf.

Engineers continued to research ways to make artificial turf better. After testing hundreds of materials, they recently began making artificial turf from coconut fiber. It's called B1K, which comes from the baseball term *batting 1.000* or *batting a thousand. Batting a thousand* means a player gets a hit every time that player is at bat. *K* comes from the Greek word kilo, which means one thousand. B1K has attracted the attention of two MLB teams. The Diamondbacks chose to use it in Chase Field because the sun is too hot there for natural grass. Artificial turf is also better for the environment because it saves water. The Texas Rangers decided to install it at their new stadium, Globe Life Field.

HITTER'S OR PITCHER'S PARK?

All baseball infields must have the same dimensions. But no MLB ballpark outfield is exactly the same as another. That's because the outfields can have different dimensions. The walls around the outfield can be set at different distances. Engineers have figured out many ways to use differences in the outfield to give advantages to hitters or pitchers.

In Game 2 of the 2010 World Series, the Texas Rangers' Ian Kinsler hit a long fly ball off San Francisco Giants pitcher Matt Cain. The ball bounced off the top of the outfield wall. But instead of bouncing out of San Francisco's AT&T Park for a homer, it bounced back onto the field. Giants outfielder Andres Torres threw the ball back to the infield, and Kinsler only reached second base. The Rangers did not score that inning and the Giants won the game. Experts say if the same ball had been hit in the Rangers' home park, it would have been a home run.

FOSSIL SURPRISE

Coors Field in Denver is the home of the Colorado Rockies. Opened in 1995, it was the first ballpark with an underground heating system. In the process of digging up the field to install the heating system, workers uncovered several intact dinosaur fossils.

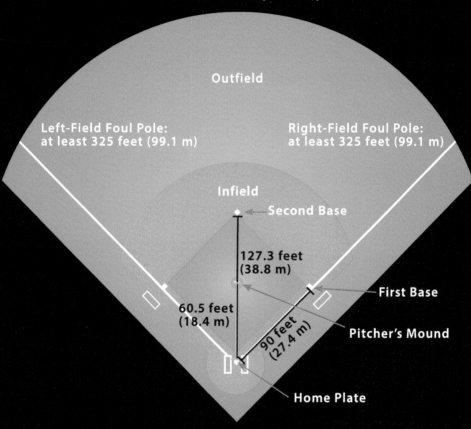

Center-Field Fence:
at least 400 feet (121.9 m)

Outfield

Left-Field Foul Pole:
at least 325 feet (99.1 m)

Right-Field Foul Pole:
at least 325 feet (99.1 m)

Infield

Second Base

127.3 feet
(38.8 m)

First Base

60.5 feet
(18.4 m)

90 feet
(27.4 m)

Pitcher's Mound

Home Plate

Baseball is the only professional sport played on fields that
vary in size from park to park. The infield diamond must have
the exact dimensions shown above. But the distance and
height of the outfield walls are different in every stadium.
Engineering choices can give advantages or disadvantages to
certain positions.

Stadium designers also think about the weather. When the Rangers' park was built in the early 1990s, engineers sunk the playing field 22 feet (6.7 m) below the level of the surrounding street. A large roofed home run porch in right field blocks the breeze. Signs and scoreboards were positioned to protect players from the wind. The goal of the engineers was to screen the wind to prevent it from changing the way the ball traveled. They didn't want the wind to give an advantage to the pitcher or the batter. They wanted to make it a neutral park. But after using the stadium, players said these design choices make the park a better place for batters.

In 2016 the Rangers unveiled plans for a new ballpark to open in 2020, just across the parking lot from their old park. During the design process, engineers found a foolproof way to handle the wind this time around— they added a retractable roof.

The high walls and barriers around Globe Life Park
protected the field from wind.

AL EAST

	W	L	GE
BOSTON	108	54	—
NEW YORK	100	62	8
TAMPA BAY	90	72	18
TORONTO	73	89	34
BALTIMORE	47	115	6

Numbers help teams keep track of their position in the standings leading up to the World Series.

5

WORLD SERIES MATHEMATICS

ath plays a big role in determining which teams go to the World Series. MLB teams play 162 games in the regular season. MLB is divided into two leagues, the American League and the National League. Each league has three divisions—East, Central, and West. There are five teams in each division. Teams within the same division play each other the most frequently. The winners of each division move up to the playoffs. There are also two wild card teams in each league. They are the teams with the best records among those that did not win their division. Eventually only two teams remain: one from the AL and one from the NL. Those teams play each other in the World Series.

Two scientists from Los Alamos National Laboratory studied the math behind the system that sends teams to the World Series. The scientists said that the 162 games does not provide enough data to ensure that the best team in each league is the winner. According to these experts, the number of games on the schedule should be about the same as the number of teams cubed. Since each league has 15 teams, that means the total number of games in a season should be 15x15x15. That means there would be 3,375 games for each league. Divide that number between 15 teams, and each team would have to play 225 games. This much data would give a more accurate result as to which team is the best of the league. But the more random results from 162 games means that sometimes underdogs make it to the World Series and win. The Florida Marlins did just this in 2003.

Florida Marlins manager Mike Redmond, *left*, and former general manager Jack McKeon celebrate the tenth anniversary of the team's 2003 World Series win.

PICKING PLAYERS AND POSITIONS

Baseball teams hire experts called scouts to watch baseball games all over the world. They look for talented players. Scouts help managers decide which players to draft or sign to contracts. Today math also influences the decision. Managers hire experts to analyze data about players. This is how they make decisions about who to choose for their team. The Los Angeles Dodgers faced the Houston Astros in the 2017 World Series. They were among the teams that leaned heavily on data and analytics to pick their players.

MLB managers also use math to decide where to position their players. Shane Jensen is a statistics expert at the University of Pennsylvania. He developed a math model that measures factors about baseball players. For example, it looks at how many runs a fielder saves or cost his team. Managers can use the model to figure out whether their players would do better at shortstop, third base, or another position. Jensen's model takes

BASEBALL STATISTICS

In 1859 sports reporter Henry Chadwick started publishing a grid of numbers with data on baseball games. It was called a box score. In the 1970s, sports fan Bill James started publishing a journal of baseball statistics. He used the data to analyze game outcomes. Today this way of using math for baseball is called sabermetrics. It is named for the Society for American Baseball Research (SABR).

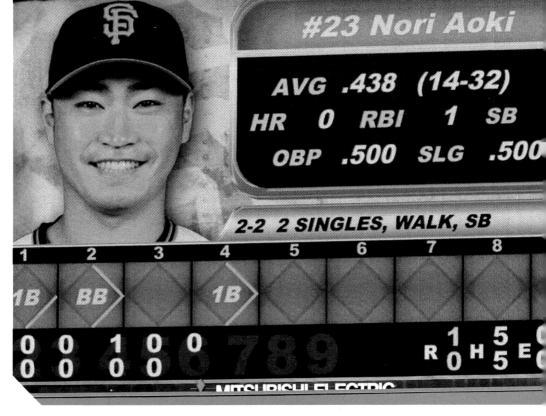

AVG .438 (14-32)
HR 0 RBI 1 SB
OBP .500 SLG .500

2-2 2 SINGLES, WALK, SB

Statistics help teams figure out each player's strengths and weaknesses. Teams can use this knowledge to give themselves the best chance of making it to the World Series.

data, such as how many times a fielder catches a ball in a certain location, and calculates the probability of that fielder's future performance.

Statistics give feedback to help managers, as well. Steve Wang is a statistician at Swarthmore College. Also a Yankees fan, he came up with a way to analyze the performance of managers. He records data such as how often a manager uses his relief pitchers, or how often he moves his players to different positions in a season. He uses this data to identify the manager's style. Then he offers information about which style would be most effective with different kinds of teams.

WHAT'S NEXT?

The World Series has gone through many changes since the first event in 1903. Baseball experts predict that games will be faster and safer due to STEM advances. Some observers think a pitch clock—already in use in some minor leagues—will be used in MLB games. A timer would allow only 20 seconds between pitches, helping to prevent long games. Better helmets or caps will be designed to protect the heads of players. New technology will monitor players' hearts and brains to make sure they are not overly stressed.

As more games are played, advances in science, technology, engineering, and math will continue to make the World Series one of America's favorite events.

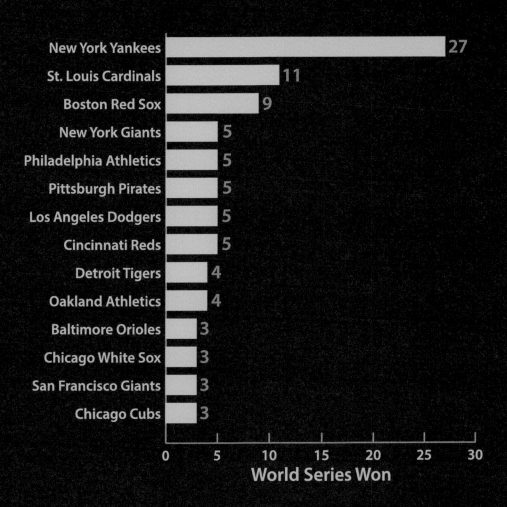

New York Yankees — 27
St. Louis Cardinals — 11
Boston Red Sox — 9
New York Giants — 5
Philadelphia Athletics — 5
Pittsburgh Pirates — 5
Los Angeles Dodgers — 5
Cincinnati Reds — 5
Detroit Tigers — 4
Oakland Athletics — 4
Baltimore Orioles — 3
Chicago White Sox — 3
San Francisco Giants — 3
Chicago Cubs — 3

World Series Won

This chart shows the teams that won three or more
World Series championships between 1903 to 2018. The
most successful team in the history of the game is the
New York Yankees. They have won more than twice the number
of World Series championships than the second-ranked
franchise, the St. Louis Cardinals.

GLOSSARY

analytics
The process of studying data to make decisions.

data
Information such as numbers.

inning
A division of a baseball game during which each team is allowed three outs while batting.

mass
A measure of how much matter is in an object.

model
A representation of a real-world thing.

momentum
A combination of speed in a certain direction and mass.

physics
The science of matter and energy and their interactions.

retractable roof
A roof that can open and close.

scout
A person who searches for someone or something.

statistics
A branch of mathematics that gathers and works to understand data such as numbers.

turf
Grass; can be natural or artificial.

underdogs
People or teams who are not expected to win.

MORE INFORMATION

BOOKS

Bechtel, Mark. *Sports Illustrated Kids Big Book of Who: Baseball.* New York: Liberty Street, 2017.

Herman, Gail. *What Is the World Series?* New York: Grosset & Dunlap, 2015.

Ventura, Marne. *STEM in Baseball.* Minneapolis, MN: Abdo Publishing, 2018.

ONLINE RESOURCES

To learn more about STEM in the World Series, visit abdobooklinks.com or scan this QR code. These links are routinely monitored and updated to provide the most current information available.

INDEX

ABOUT THE AUTHOR

Marne Ventura is the author of many books for kids, both fiction and nonfiction. She enjoys writing about science, technology, engineering, math, arts and crafts, and the lives of creative people. A former elementary school teacher, she holds a master's degree in education from the University of California. Marne and her husband live on the central coast of California.